HAPPY

by Howie Dewin

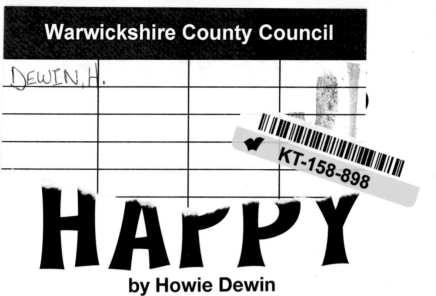

ISBN 978-1-338-25647-5

10 9 8 7 6 5 4 3 2 1   18 19 20 21 22

Printed in the U.S.A.   40

First printing 2018

Book design by Theresa Venezia

Contents

Introduction

Welcome to the Unikingdom!

It's a beautiful day! I love beautiful days! I'm Princess Unikitty and I'm sooooo happy you're here! Yay! There's so much fun to have and games to play! If you're not happy right now, I'm going to help you fix that! It's time to get happy, happier, happiest!!! Wheeeeee!

There is nothing in the world I love more than loving everything in the world! My friends, my family, my kingdom, the sky, big trees, fluffy clouds, and tea parties—I love it all!

The only thing I don't like is anything that is the opposite of NICE and HAPPY and FRIENDLY and KIND and SPARKLY and FLUFFY and CUTE!

OOOOEEEEEEEAAAAAHHHHH! CUTE THINGS!!!

I looooove cute things! Don't you?

I hope you are as happy as me. But if you aren't, just stick with me! I am here to help you figure out how to be as happy as you can possibly be.

How many ways can you say Hi-EEEEE?

Hi!

Hi-eeeee!

Hello!

He-e-e-e-llo-o-o-o!

H-H-H-H-H-idey-Hodey-Hey!!!

Howdy!

Ho-o-o-o-wdy!

Howd-eeeeeeeey!

Hey-Hey-Hey!

Say it however you want—just be sure you say it a lot! It really cheers people up when someone says HI-EEEEEEEE! And that's our goal, because the first step to being happy is to help other people feel happy!

Unikitty's Guide to:

Discovering Your Inner Happy!

I LOVE HAPPINESS!

Nothing makes me happier than happiness. For everyone! Everywhere! I want the whole world to live in the Land of Happiness!

But sometimes it takes a little work to get to happiness. You might have to hike through a little bit of boredom or a tiny bit of sadness. But, that's okay! In fact, it's great! Because if you let yourself get through those feelings, then they won't stand in the way of happiness! The fact is, you need to feel all kinds of emotions if you want to feel BIG Happiness.

I will admit I have a little (VERY LITTLE!) problem with my temper. Sometimes it takes charge inside me a little (JUST A LITTLE!). But I always keep my eye on the ball! I always try to make my heart bigger than my temper. The best way to do that is to let myself feel a little (JUST A LITTLE!) frustration or boredom or sadness so that those feelings don't get in the way of my HAPPINESS!

Discovering Your Inner Happy!

YAY, Sparkle Matter!!

I **LOVE SPARKLE MATTER!** It's that great stuff that pops out of your head when you have strong feelings.

There are **Happy Sparticles** (My Favorite!) and **Negative Sparkle Matter**.

Everybody's Sparkle Matter is different because we all have different things that make us feel happy or sad or confused or bored and so on and so on. So it's important to know what your personal Sparkle Matter looks like and that depends on knowing what kinds of things make your Happy Sparticles pop out of your head and what things bring out your Negative Sparkles.

Everybody is different, and their Sparkle Matter is unique!

Discovering Your Inner Happy!

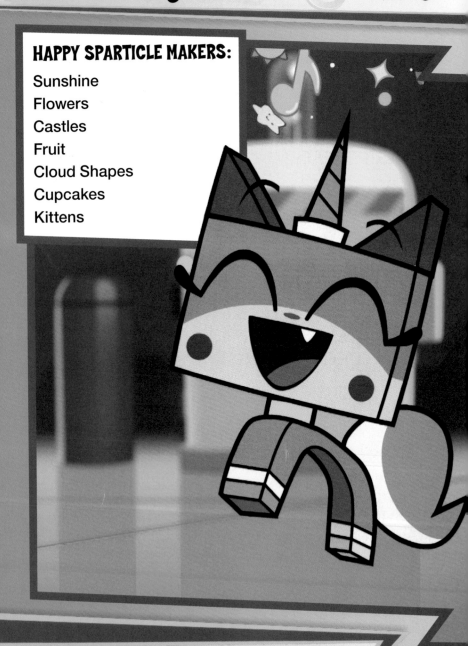

HAPPY SPARTICLE MAKERS:

Sunshine
Flowers
Castles
Fruit
Cloud Shapes
Cupcakes
Kittens

NEGATIVE SPARKLE MATTER MAKERS:

Not Being Nice
Not Being Polite
Name-Calling
Interrupting
Mean Tricks

Unikitty's Guide to:

Making Happy Friends!

Making Happy Friends!

I**LOVE FRIENDS!** New friends! Old friends! Friends I haven't met yet! It's all good to me because FRIENDS are what make good times great and great times out-of-this-world fan-fun-tastic!

Finding FRIENDS who will turn your great times into fan-fun-tastic times is about asking a few important questions when you meet a new friend. (You can also ask these questions about yourself just to make sure you're being the best friend you can be, too!)

Wheeeeeee!

Here are my HAPPY FRIEND QUESTIONS:

- Do I have things in common with this person? (Do we both explode with Happy Sparticles over the same things?)

- Does this person care about other people's feelings? (Does this person help other people make Happy Sparticles?)

- Does this person make sure no one feels left out? (Does this person try to make less Negative Sparkle Matter in the world?)

- Does this person help other people when they need help? (Do their Happy Sparticles explode when they help someone even if it means doing something that might not be much fun?)

If you can answer YES! to these questions about your friends, then you have AMAZING friends! And if you can answer YES! about yourself—YOU ARE AMAZING, TOO!

I am sooooo happy that my friends are AH-MAAAAA-ZING! ZING! ZING! Allow me to introduce them!

Making Happy Friends!

Puppycorn isn't just my BEST FRIEND . . . he's my BROTHER! How cool is that? Nobody knows FUN like Puppycorn. Boredom doesn't stand a shot! He's the only friend I know who might have more energy than me! WOW! WOW! WOW!

My Sparkle Matter
is a paper clip.

Richard or "Rick" (if you're lucky enough to be his friend) is really old and has learned just about EVERYTHING! So he gives great advice! Plus, he would do ANYTHING to make sure I'm okay and that my life goes smoothly. He cares more about me and Puppycorn (and all his other friends) than he does about himself!

Making Happy Friends!

Dr. Fox is a brilliant, great friend! I mean, really! She's a total genius and she uses her smarts to do really cool experiments! She always figures out how to solve our problems and it usually includes making things explode or expand or get more sparkly or shinier or fluffier or brighter . . . well, you get the point! She makes things more fun in a smart kinda way!! What could EVER be wrong about that?

Hawkodile is that rare combination of boffo bodyguard and fabulous friend. He's always one step ahead and has everything under control. He does what he has to to keep his friends safe. Plus . . . he calls me Princess!

I practice fighting in the dark in case the sun disappears.

Making Happy Friends!

Concerned!

Common Interests!

Helpful!

Caring!

Fun Stuff with Friends:

Eating Snacks

Playing Video Games

Listening to Sick Beats

Playing Soccer

Surfing

Marching in Parades

Roller-Skating

MY LIFE IS AWESOME BECAUSE OF

YOU!

Unikitty's Guide to:

Dealing with the Big Unhappy!

Dealing with the Big Unhappy!

I do **NOT** like UNhappy.

No way! No how!

But HAPPY is mightier than UNHAPPY. You just have to remember that UNHAPPY is tricky and will try to sneak up on you. So stay alert and keep HAPPY all around you so UNHAPPY can't steal your Sparkles!

There will always be UNHAPPY people.

EXAMPLE: Master Frown. (AAUUGGHH! Master Frown is SUCH a meanie!)

But I take a deep breath, think sparkly thoughts, and then try to turn their UNHAPPY HAPPY before they turn my HAPPY UNHAPPY!

That's what I do every time I go to Frown Town. (AAUUGGHH! The MOST depressing place in the world!)

Not surprisingly, it's home to Master Frown. (AAUUGGHH! He makes everyone cry!!)

But I just stay focused and make sure HAPPY wins. No matter what!

STEP ONE to making sure HAPPY always beats UNHAPPY is to make sure you don't let UNHAPPY sneak up on you. And to make sure that doesn't happen, you have to know what UNHAPPY looks like!

So turn the page and meet UNHAPPY! (Boooo! Hisss! AAUUGGHH!)

Dealing with the Big Unhappy!

Life according to Master Frown:

Life speeds by. You get a job. You never play. The end.

Life according to Unikitty:

Have you ever seen anything so beautiful?

Master Frown's Quick List of Fun Things to Do When You Only Have a Minute . . .

- Lose someone's place in a long book
- Drop a water balloon on someone's head
- Knock ice cream off a baby's cone

Dealing with the Big Unhappy!

Name: Master Frown

Occupation: Being a meanie

Home: Frown Town

Greatest Passion: Making people cry

Greatest Achievement: Being voted Most Likely to Ruin Your Day

Rule #1: There's always time to make just one more person frown.

Name: Brock

Occupation: Being Master Frown's roommate

Home: Master Frown's apartment in Frown Town

Greatest Passion: Chilling out

Greatest Achievement: Getting Master Frown to clean his room

Rule #1: Do not offer cookies to Master Frown's archnemesis.

Dealing with the Big Unhappy!

Unikitty has Master Frown. I have . . . the Eagle-ator!

Name: Eagle-ator
Occupation: Defeating Hawkodile and getting those Sweet Shades
Home: Action Forest
Greatest Passion: Those Sweet Shades
Greatest Achievement: Getting those Sweet Shades
Rule #1: Always believe you deserve those Sweet Shades

Dealing with the Big Unhappy!

(Un)Welcome to Frown Town . . . The Most Depressing Place in the World!

Frown Town is the epicenter of sadness, the beating heart of gloom—Master Frown's apartment.

Travel Tip: If you want to stay happy, stay out of Frown Town!

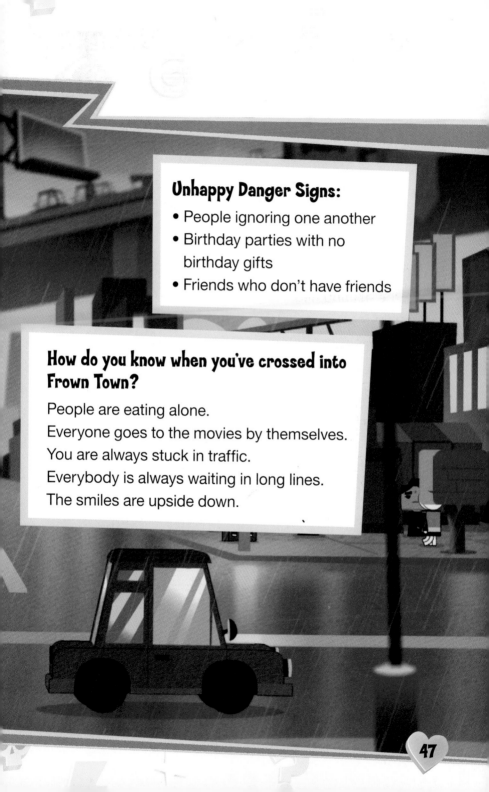

Unhappy Danger Signs:

- People ignoring one another
- Birthday parties with no birthday gifts
- Friends who don't have friends

How do you know when you've crossed into Frown Town?

People are eating alone.

Everyone goes to the movies by themselves.

You are always stuck in traffic.

Everybody is always waiting in long lines.

The smiles are upside down.

Dealing with the Big Unhappy!

Unikitty's Guide to:

Let Your Happiness Shine!

SHINE! SHINE! SHINE!

There's only one thing to do when you're happy and that is SHINE! Because then your happiness becomes contagious and people everywhere will catch it. Pretty soon, the whole world will catch it. Happy Sparticles will cover the globe! WHEEEEEEEEE!

So get busy doing HAPPY things for yourself and for others! HAPPY will spread like wildfire!

How am I happy? Oh, in so many ways! The only thing that could make me happier is to SHARE THE HAPPY with you!

So—Introducing . . . Princess Unikitty's Eight Great Ways to Let Your HAPPY Shine!

Let Your Happiness Shine!

#1 Be Silly Whenever Possible

(such as making funny noises)

Robot Noises: Boop! Bop! Beep!

Dance Sounds: Oontz! Oontz!

Rocket Ship Attack Noises: Bew! Bew-bew!

Let Your Happiness Shine!

#2 Play Dress Up!

Ghost!

Body Builder!

Let Your Happiness Shine!

#3 Fix a Problem for a Friend!

Being nice is the best!

Let Your Happiness Shine!

#4 Play WITH Your Friends . . . Not AGAINST them!

I'm gonna win this sooo hard!

Let Your Happiness Shine!

#5 Have a Tea Party!

You will need:

- Tasty tea for sipping
- Cakes for nibbling
- Best friends for sharing

Let Your Happiness Shine!

#6 Don't Forget to Let Yourself
Know That You Like You!

Let Your Happiness Shine!

#7 Celebrate Like You Mean It!

Let Your Happiness Shine!

#8 Let People Know When You Love Them!

Let Your Happiness Shine!

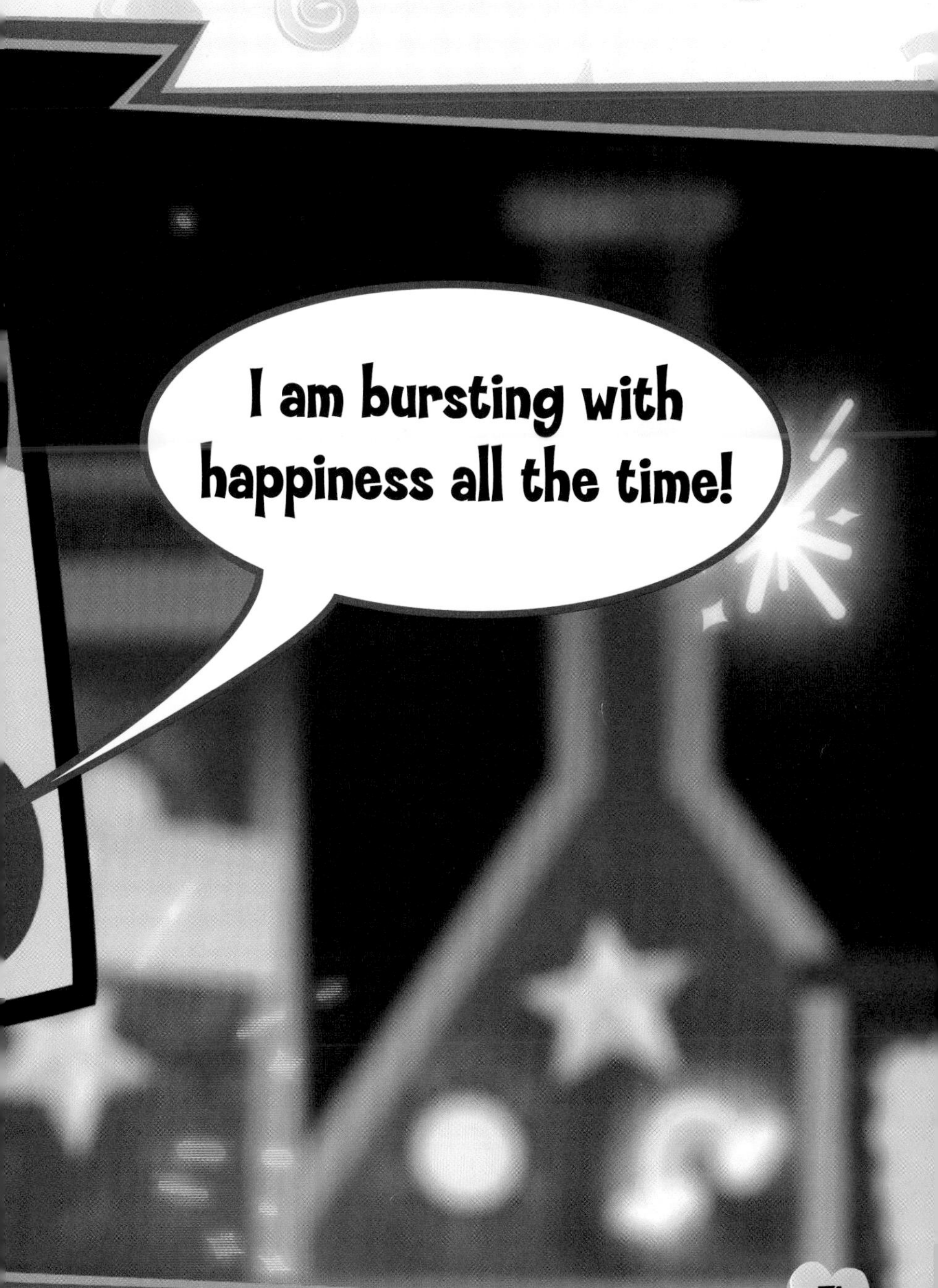
I am bursting with happiness all the time!

Smilin' 'n' Stylin' Your Happy Look!

Smile with style!

That's what I say!
Sometimes it's just the silly little things that make a moment happy. It might not feel big and important, but that doesn't mean it isn't.

> Get dressed up!
> Tell a friend a joke!
> Fix your hair!
> Take a ride!
> Send someone a postcard!
> Rearrange your room!
> Draw a picture for someone you love!
> Clean your windows until they sparkle!
> Take a dog for a walk!
> Sing a song!

I know. Those are all just little things. But sometimes all it takes is a little thing to cheer someone up (including you!). Anytime you take a little extra time to care about someone (including you!) or do something special for someone (including you!), the world gets a teeny bit happier.

So, big or small, go for it! As long as you are making smiles and not frowns, it's all good!

Whoa! I look
GOOOOD!
This is FUN!

Smilin' 'n' Stylin'!

[Unikitty:] when life gets tough
don't you get down
you gotta turn that frown
upside down!

[Hawkodile:]
my name is Hawkodile
and i'm hear to say
lifting and training makes my day!

Smilin' 'n' Stylin'!

We're always happy when we're rollin' up in our cool vehicles!

WE HAVE TO DO IT OUR WAY!

Unikitty's Guide to:

Battling the Big Unhappy!

Battling the Big Unhappy!

It's time to get serious. (BUT JUST FOR A SECOND!) You are ready to move to the next level in your happiness training. Let me hear you say, "I'm ready!"

Okay!

In the name of happiness and smiles and all things SPARKLY, it's time to face a few tough facts.

At some point, you will have to do battle against the forces that want to crush happiness.

That can mean people—like Master Frown and Brock or the Eagle-ator—or it can mean your own feelings—like being BORED!

Either way, you need to train for that battle like the superhero you are. You must stand up to the enemies of happiness! So, since it's always best to learn from a Master, I'm turning this section over to my friend—The Big H!

Battling the Big Unhappy!

Defeat any enemy!

Crash through
windows in slow motion!

Hawkodile's Credo!

No matter what you want to do with your life, it is totally worth becoming an action hero! It teaches you how to do so many cool things!

Look really cool in front of explosions!

Eat my dust!

Deliver the best one-liners!

Gotta carbo-load!

These fists need power!

I'm not heavy. I'm dense!

Battling the Big Unhappy!

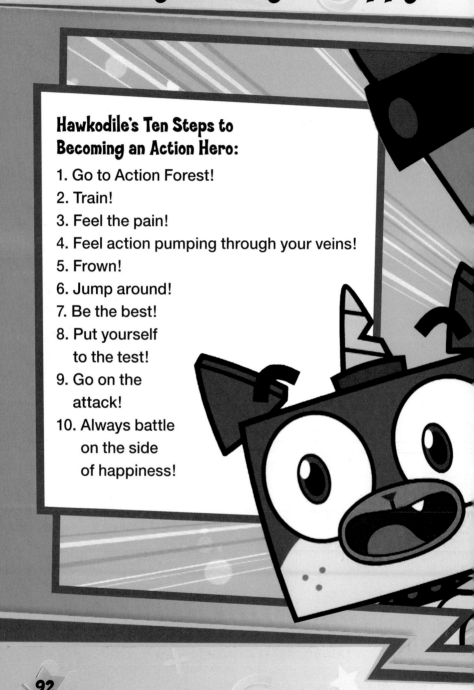

Hawkodile's Ten Steps to Becoming an Action Hero:

1. Go to Action Forest!
2. Train!
3. Feel the pain!
4. Feel action pumping through your veins!
5. Frown!
6. Jump around!
7. Be the best!
8. Put yourself to the test!
9. Go on the attack!
10. Always battle on the side of happiness!

And make sure you get your catchphrase action hero nsame!

The Loose Cannon!

The Tired Veteran!

There's a time for hugs and a time for karate.

Fisticuffs it is!

Battling the Big Unhappy!

When the happiness-stomping forces are feelings—like boredom—you have to be ready in other ways! What's the best way to beat back boredom?

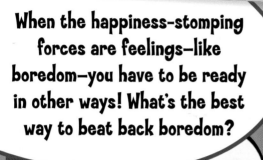

ACTIVATE!

That's right, Puppycorn! Make your to-do list!

Boredom-Busting To-Do List:
- March in Parade
- Schedule Tea Party
- Go to the Disco
- Ride the Roller Coaster

Mad?

Express your frustrations constructively so you can move on!

Sad? Help fix a problem for someone else!

You gotta get your priorities straight! "Hi" first. "Boring Stuff" second.

Unikitty's Guide to:

Making Your Happy Place!

Making Your Happy Place!

I LOVE MY HAPPY PLACE!

Do you know where your happy place is? It's the spot where you feel safe and happy. It's where you have lots of fun and great adventures. It's where you get to be with the people you love the most!

The most important thing about your happy place is that it is YOUR happy place and nobody else's! It should be just right for you! It should be filled with the things that make YOU feel happy and comfortable and it doesn't have to feel "just right" for anyone else!

Everyone has their very own happy place.

Everyone has their very own happy place.

Everyone has their very own happy place.

I have to say it over and over because it's really important and sometimes I forget it. Here's what I learned: Don't try to make your happy place look like your friend's!

Happy Place Rule #1: You Be YOU!

You know what my happy place is? I'll give you one guess!

Making Your Happy Place!

UNIKINGDOM!

I LOVE BEING THE PRINCESS OF UNIKINGDOM BECAUSE I LOVE UNIKINGDOM!

It's the perfect happy place!

I mean . . . it's MY perfect happy place.

It's filled with my friends and family, there's always fun stuff to do, and everybody loves being happy as much as I do!

Giant Me Fountain

Perfect Tea Party Location

Castle

Toy District

Beach

Ice Cream Flavor of the Month Spot

Genius Friend's
Laboratory

Making Your Happy Place!

Prince Puppycorn's kingdom! Hello, happy place!!

Pizza for every meal

Everyone lives in bouncy castles

Fireworks all the time

Roller coaster highways

Pay for things with high fives

Home of many action heroes

Lots of places to practice cool action skills

Birthplace of the sweet shades

Where sensei lives

Action Forest! Where else?

Great training dojo

Making Your Happy Place!

You don't have to be a rocket scientist to know my happy place is my laboratory!

- Lots of beakers, flasks, and test tubes
- Biggest collection of Sparkle Matter
- Ultra-powerful microscope
- Important diplomas and certificates
- Perfect cupcake recipe
- Site of my greatest experiments

My room: the Cleaning Closet. There is no better place in the world.

- Highly effective brooms
- Very absorbent mops
- Massive collection of spot removers
- Finest feather dusters
- Wide range of soap buckets
- Ultra-microfiber cleaning cloths

Making Your Happy Place!

Stay positive! Everything works out in the end!

All Different Kinds of Happy!

CLEANING!

INVENTING!

PROTECTING!

CHEWING STUFF!

All Different Kinds of Happy!

Don't forget—**your way of feeling happy** might not be your friends' ways of feeling happy. Everybody gets to find their own kind of happiness. So listen to your friends when they tell you what they like and don't like!

Let's not play near power lines!

I would prefer not to share lunch.

Let's take separate vehicles.

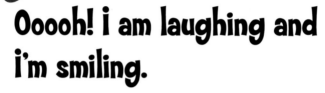

Ooooh! i am laughing and i'm smiling.

Oh, oh, and i see you laughing too!

Nothing can make me say it was a bad day.

Can't make me say that!

Bye-eeeeeee! Farewell!

Rainbows and Unicorns! Rainbows and Unicorns! Oooooooh! I HATE saying good-bye!

There is nothing in the world I love more than loving everything in the world! My friends, my family, my kingdom, the sky, big trees, fluffy clouds, and tea parties—I love it all!

But we cannot be sad. Be happy because we met one another!

Farewell!

Fun! Coming Soon . . .